DOM PAUL BELLOT

Architect and Monk

Dom Paul Bellot (1876–1944). Frontispiece from *Propos d'un bâtisseur du Bon Dieu* (1949).

DOM PAUL BELLOT

Architect and Monk

and the publication of

Propos d'un bâtisseur du Bon Dieu 1949

PETER WILLIS

ELYSIUM PRESS PUBLISHERS

NEWCASTLE UPON TYNE

1996

Reprinted with amendments from
British Journal of Canadian Studies
Volume II, number 1 (1996), pp. 90–124
published by the British Association for Canadian Studies
21 George Square, Edinburgh EH8 9LD, Scotland

ISBN 0 904712 03 6

Published by
ELYSIUM PRESS PUBLISHERS
5 FENWICK CLOSE, JESMOND
NEWCASTLE UPON TYNE NEI 7RU, UK

Printed by
DOPPLER PRESS, BRENTWOOD, ESSEX
Cover design by
REDLETTER, EDINBURGH

CONTENTS

PREFACE

Dom Paul Bellot is one of the most interesting yet unrecognised architects of the 20th century. Born in Paris, and trained there at the École des Beaux-Arts, he became a Benedictine monk and subsequently designed religious buildings in Belgium, England, France, the Netherlands and Portugal.

Moving to Canada in 1937, and trapped there by the Second World War, Bellot assisted in the completion of the dome of the Oratoire Saint-Joseph in Montreal and built the first stage of the monastery of Saint-Benoît-du-Lac in Quebec, where he is buried. His architecture demonstrates a dramatic and powerful use of concrete and polychromatic brickwork, as well as an inventive exploration of light and proportional systems.

The major published statement of Bellot's ideas is contained in his volume *Propos d'un bâtisseur du Bon Dieu* which came out posthumously in Montreal in 1949 and was based on lectures he gave in Canada in 1934. A study of these lectures, focusing particularly on Bellot's references to Viollet-le-Duc, Le Corbusier and Jacques Maritain, and linking them to the writings of Saint Thomas Aquinas, is the subject of this present book. It originally appeared in April 1996 as an article in the *British Journal of Canadian Studies* (volume 11, number 1, pp. 90–124), and is now published separately by Elysium Press through the courtesy of the journal's Editor, Colin Nicholson of the University of Edinburgh. I am greatly indebted to the Assistant Editor, Jodie Robson, for her dedication and enthusiasm in preparing the text and illustrations and seeing the project through the press. Copy-editing was the responsibility of Ivor Normand, the journal's Editorial Assistant, and the cover design is by John-Paul Shirreffs of the Edinburgh designers, RedLetter.

My principal academic debts appear in the Acknowledgements and Notes which follow. To these I should add my wife Jenny, who accompanied me on sorties to archives, churches and monasteries as we traced the footsteps of Dom Bellot in England, France and Canada; in particular, our visits to his last resting place in the cemetery of the abbey of Saint-Benoît-du-Lac will never be forgotten.

PETER WILLIS

ACKNOWLEDGEMENTS

Preparation of this study was made possible by the generosity of the Canadian High Commission, which gave me a Faculty Research Award in 1994 to enable me to visit buildings by Bellot and to work in libraries and archives in Canada. Other financial assistance came from Newcastle University, the Allen R. Hite Art Institute at the University of Louisville, and the Commission of European Communities in Brussels which made a joint award under its Kaleidoscope scheme to the Department of Architecture, Newcastle University, the Archives d'Architecture Moderne, Brussels, and the Institut Français d'Architecture, Paris.

For academic support, I am grateful in particular to Claude Bergeron of Laval University, Andrew Fairbairn of Newcastle University, Dom Charles Fitzsimons OSB (the librarian at Quarr Abbey) and Dom Jean Rochon OSB (the archivist at the abbey of Saint-Benoît-du-Lac), all of whom read my text in draft. David Jasper, formerly of Durham University and now of Glasgow University, was enthusiastic throughout. Valuable assistance also came from Suze Bakker, the late Peter Burton, Maurice Culot, Charlotte Ellis, Sheridan Gilley, Mary Jones, Martin Meade and Nicole Tardif-Painchaud.

Apart from offering me extensive personal help, Christian Decotignie gave me free access to his pioneering unpublished thesis, 'Une architecture religieuse. Dom Paul Bellot (1876–1944)' (Ecole d'architecture de Lille et des Régions Nord, 1989).

For bibliographical assistance I thank Ruth Kamen, Robert Elwall and Julian Osley at the British Architectural Library in London, Janet Parks at the Avery Library at Columbia University in New York, Jan van der Wateren at the National Art Library at the Victoria and Albert Museum, Susan Day at the library of the Institut Français d'Architecture in Paris, the staff of the Robinson Library, Newcastle University, and Phyllis Lambert, Paul Chénier, Robert Desaulniers, Renata Guttman and Michèle Picard at the Centre Canadien d'Architecture in Montreal.

LIST OF PLATES

DOM PAUL BELLOT
Architect and Monk
and the publication of
Propos d'un bâtisseur du Bon Dieu 1949

Just over fifty years ago, on 5 July 1944, the architect and monk Dom Paul Bellot died in Quebec City. He was 68, and as a priest of the Order of St Benedict (OSB) had spent much of his life designing religious buildings for the Benedictines. In addition, he had expounded his theories of architecture in talks and publications, culminating in the book *Propos d'un bâtisseur du Bon Dieu*, which came out posthumously in Montreal in 1949 and was based on lectures which he had given in Canada in 1934 (Plate 1). As the most extensive published statement of Bellot's ideas on architecture, the *Propos* deserves our careful attention, but any study of it must begin by relating it to Bellot's background and architecture.[1]

Biographical Context
Paul Louis Denis Bellot was born on 7 June 1876 at 21 rue du Cherche-Midi in Paris, his father Paul Eugène Bellot being described as a *'vérificateur en bâtiment'*, in other words a kind of surveyor.[2] From 1894–1901, Dom Paul Bellot studied architecture at the École des Beaux-Arts in Paris, but in 1902 he joined the Benedictine community of Solesmes which had left France as a result of the French anti-clerical laws of 1901. The monks from Solesmes had settled at Appuldurcombe House on the Isle of Wight, and here Bellot was clothed as a postulant on 6 October 1902 and subsequently made his monastic profession on 29 May 1904. He was ordained priest on 10 June 1911 at the nearby Quarr Abbey, which he himself had started to build in 1907 and to which the community had moved in 1908. Dom Paul Bellot's younger brother Georges Bellot (1879–1963), an artist, designer and illustrator, was also a monk at Quarr and later at Solesmes.[3]

At the École des Beaux-Arts, Bellot had been in the atelier of Marcel-Noël Lambert (1847–1928), professor of stereometry, and under Lambert's direction gained his *diplôme d'architecture* in 1900.[4] In 1901, Bellot undertook three further projects, receiving a medal that year for a design for *Un conservatoire régional des arts et métiers*. Bellot's training at the École followed a rigorous system with strict rules and set requirements and a firm commitment to classicism. Nonetheless, his final diploma scheme – a design for a *Maison de famille et cercle français à Madrid*, exhibited at the Paris Salon of 1901 – displays a pronounced use of colour and a Spanish Romanesque idiom.[5]

The ethos of the École des Beaux-Arts has parallels with the Rule of St Benedict, notably the shared beliefs that the past can teach much that is relevant for the present and that the freedom of the spirit must be restrained by discipline.

Indeed, the acceptance of discipline is itself a step towards freedom. As Bellot himself defined it in the *Propos*, his aim was 'innover selon la tradition'. For, he concluded,

> c'est en étudiant et en méditant l'art des belles époques, que nous serons armés pour reprendre la tradition de la vraie beauté et alors, comme l'a dit saint Benoît, le patriarche des moines d'Occident, 'Dieu sera glorifié en toutes choses'. (*Propos* 55)

Small wonder, then, as we shall see, that Bellot provided a theological basis for his architectural theories.

In 1906, Bellot, who surely never expected to practise again as an architect, was asked to design buildings for those monks from Solesmes who had escaped to Oosterhout, near Breda, in the Netherlands. Bellot's departure from Appuldurcombe to Oosterhout marked the beginning of his independent professional career. Shortly afterwards, Bellot was called back to Appuldurcombe, which the monks were due to leave in 1908, and in 1907–14 erected residential accommodation and the church for them at Quarr Abbey (Plates 2–3). Subsequently, Bellot constructed monastic and educational buildings and parish churches in France, Belgium and the Netherlands. This work went largely uncelebrated until 1927 and the publication of the book *Une œuvre d'architecture moderne, par Dom Paul Bellot, osb*, which effectively gave an *imprimatur* to the first stage of Bellot's career as an architect.[6]

Published in French, Dutch and English, and emanating initially from the abbey of Mont Vierge at Wépion, in Belgium, this has an introductory essay by the sculptor Henri Charlier (1883–1975), who had already provided a statue of the Virgin Mary at Solesmes and who was to be one of Bellot's most fervent champions in both Europe and Canada; indeed, in 1928 the abbey of Mont Vierge also brought out a similar book on Charlier called *Les tailles directes d'Henri Charlier, statuaire*, which included a catalogue of Charlier's sculpture and an essay by the Abbé Georges Duret entitled 'Théorie de l'art chrétien'. Furthermore, descriptions of Bellot's buildings were provided by the architect Maurice Storez (1875–1959), the founder in 1917 of the group of Catholic artists known as *L'Arche* which included, as well as Bellot and Charlier, the architect Eugène Stassin, the liturgical designer Fernand Py, and the stained-glass artist Valentine Reyre. In the promotion of its ideas, *L'Arche* was aided by Père Abel Fabre (1872–1929), the historian and art critic,[7] and by the journal *L'artisan liturgique* which published two issues in 1929 and 1933 respectively devoted to showing the range of activity (including embroidery and goldsmithing) of members of the group.[8] As Storez explained, *L'Arche* was not committed to any preceding style, but rather sought new forms of expression based on rational principles, embracing new materials and rejecting imitation. These were set in the context of changes in the rôle of the arts in Roman Catholic worship and liturgy. Indeed, as *Une œuvre d'architecture moderne* was being published, Bellot was collaborating with Storez and other members of *L'Arche* at the church of Saint-Chrysole at Comines, on the Belgian–French border.

CAHIERS D'ART

ARCA

IV

PROPOS D'UN BÂTISSEUR
DU BON DIEU

DOM PAUL BELLOT, o.s.b.

ÉDITIONS FIDES — MONTRÉAL

PLATE 1: Titlepage from *Propos d'un bâtisseur du Bon Dieu* (1949).

Not merely does *Une œuvre d'architecture moderne* offer supportive statements by Charlier and Storez, it also presents powerful images of the buildings themselves in photographs and drawings, some in colour. These are of Quarr Abbey and six locations in the Netherlands: the abbey of Saint-Paul, Oosterhout; the parish church, rectory and school at Noordhoek; the sisters' kindergarten and convent at Bavel; the enlargement of the parish church at Heerlen; the college and chapel of the Augustinian Fathers at Eindhoven; and the cemetery chapel at Bloemendaal. Clearly demonstrated here are the powerful characteristics of Bellot's architecture: the use of parabolic arches and polychromatic brickwork (Plate 4), the experimentation with reinforced concrete, the introduction of dramatic lighting, the spatial invention and the freedom from overt historical constraints. Charlier, in his introductory essay, expresses no doubts about Bellot's gifts: 'C'est un homme de métier, c'est un constructeur; il est lui aussi, dans un certain sens, l'homme d'un matériau, la brique, dont il tire tout ce qu'elle peut donner' (p. 9). Charlier sums up his impression of Bellot when he ends his remarks with the observation that 'la France a fait ainsi un missionnaire de celui de ces architectes qui rappelle le mieux les maîtres d'œuvre de nos anciennes cathédrales' (p. 13). It is a view which Storez endorses elsewhere in the book.

PLATE 2: Quarr Abbey, Isle of Wight. Exterior showing (from left) porch, church and campanile by Dom Bellot.

PLATE 3: Quarr Abbey, Isle of Wight. Detail of entrance to monastery by Dom Bellot.

The publication of *Une œuvre d'architecture moderne* in both Europe and the USA meant that Bellot's work became known internationally, first through book reviews and then through coverage in magazines. In the Netherlands, B. J. Koldewey published three articles in 1929 in *Het Roomsh Katholiek Bouwblad* entitled 'Het Werk van Père Bellot', to which Bellot responded.[9] The English edition was published in Boston as *A Modern Architectural Work, by Dom Paul Bellot, OSB* and welcomed on the other side of the Atlantic. In the USA, *The Catholic World*, published in New York, expressed the hope that 'Dom Bellot's efforts will influence future work of an ecclesiastical nature and free us from the shackles of sham archaeology'.[10] Similarly, two eminent American architects reviewed the book enthusiastically, Ralph Adams Cram in *The New York Times* observing that the book was 'most interesting, unexpected and altogether stimulating',[11] and Barry Byrne in *The Commonweal* noting that 'the work of Dom Bellot is probably the most significant contribution to Christian architecture now current'.[12] It is not without interest that these reviews by Cram and Byrne were quoted approvingly by Gérard Petit CSC (under the pseudonym Gilmard) in his book *La vraie France*, published in Montreal by Éditions Fides in 1941.[13]

PLATE 4: Details of bay at Eindhoven, Netherlands, for the Augustinian Fathers, from *Une œuvre d'architecture moderne, par Dom Paul Bellot, OSB* (1927), plate 94.

PLATE 5: Church of the Immaculate Conception, Audincourt. Plate from *Propos d'un bâtisseur du Bon Dieu* (1949) showing chancel by Dom Bellot.

The years following the appearance of *Une œuvre d'architecture moderne* saw both the expansion of Bellot's commissions and an increase in the coverage of his architecture in periodicals. The ensuing decade witnessed extensive work by Bellot in France, including extensions to the abbey at Wisques, the church of the Immaculate Conception at Audincourt (Plate 5), the church of Notre-Dame-des-Trévois at Troyes (Plate 6), the Monastère des Tourelles at Montpellier, the priory of Sainte-Bathilde at Vanves, the church of Saint-Joseph at Annecy (Haute-Savoie), the cloister and library at Solesmes, and extensions to the monastery of La Pierre-qui-Vire, near Avallon. Charlier continued to champion Bellot in this period, publishing articles on his work in *L'artisan liturgique* in 1929 and 1933, and in *Liturgical Arts* in 1935. Others were to follow.[14] It seems too that Bellot himself was a strong promoter of his own architecture and the values which it represented.

Canadian Lectures

The first contact between Dom Bellot and Canada was through the architect Adrien Dufresne (1904–82) from Quebec, who had encountered Bellot's work in various publications available in Canada in the 1920s.[15] Dufresne wrote to Maurice Storez in 1926, and later corresponded with Dom Bellot whom he met in Paris and Wisques in 1930; in 1932 Dufresne organised an exhibition on Bellot in Canada under the patronage of Laval University. Meanwhile in 1931–2 the architect Edgar Courchesne (1903–79), also from Quebec, who had studied at the École des Arts Décoratifs in Paris, spent eight months working with Bellot at Wisques and subsequently published articles in Canada which acted as a prelude to Bellot's Montreal lectures.[16]

Through his friendship with Dufresne and Courchesne, and stimulated by the publication of his work, Bellot was initially approached about a visit to Canada by Père Henri-Paul Bergeron of the Congrégation de Sainte-Croix (CSC).[17] Subsequently, he was invited officially by the Institut Scientifique Franco-Canadien, and he duly lectured at the École des Beaux-Arts in Montreal between 19 February and 9 March 1934, and later in Quebec City, Sherbrooke and elsewhere.[18] Bellot would have prepared his lectures at Wisques, and the archives there contain annotated copies of the lectures as well as an extensive collection of black-and-white slides which Bellot must have used.[19]

There were nine lectures in all, presented in two series under the general title of 'L'architecture religieuse moderne' with the subtitle 'Innover en architecture selon la juste tradition'; the first series of four lectures was called 'Questions d'esthétique' and the second series of five 'Questions de technique'. Bellot was enthusiastically received in Canada, and newspapers carried detailed reports of his lectures, frequently with photographs of Bellot and his hosts, who included Charles Maillard, Director of the École des Beaux-Arts in Montreal, as well as Dufresne, Courchesne, Ernest Cormier and other eminent Canadian architects.[20]

Newspaper articles provide a significant commentary on Bellot's reception. The week before Bellot's first lecture, for instance, Lucien Desbiens, writing in

PLATE 6: Church of Notre-Dame-des-Trévois, Troyes. Plate from *Propos d'un bâtisseur du Bon Dieu* (1949) showing nave by Dom Bellot.

Le Devoir, welcomed him to Montreal. Meeting Bellot, he remarked, 'nous nous trouvons en présence d'un homme très gai, aux yeux pétillants de malice, au sourire facile'. Bellot, said Desbiens, was primarily a 'poète de la brique', using brickwork audaciously. 'Fils du pays de la couleur', Desbiens wrote, 'Dom Bellot accorde une place de premier plan à la couleur et réalise des symphonies polychromes des plus séduisantes'.[21]

PLATE 7: Oratory of Saint-Joseph, Montreal. Entrance front with dome completed by Dom Bellot, Parent and Tourville.

Once the lectures were under way, the press reported them extensively and with enthusiasm. In an article entitled 'Un art canadien', the newspaper *La Presse* commented on the wider implications of Dom Bellot's observations. 'Vous pouvez', *La Presse* reported Bellot as saying, 'vous Canadiens, en restant vous-mêmes, des catholiques et des Canadiens, contribuer à la création d'un art bien à vous, par votre encouragement aux artistes'.[22] Robert Rumilly, in *Le Petit Journal*, wrote: 'Exilé pendant 26 ans par les tristes lois laïques, Dom Bellot s'est fait pèlerin de la foi, pèlerin de l'idéal, pèlerin de l'art'. Rumilly greatly admired Bellot's presentation: 'l'éloquence du moine-professeur est, dans la simplicité, directe, irrésistible'. French-Canadians, moreover, could draw especial satisfaction from Bellot's success: 'Nous avons un plaisir particulier', commented Rumilly, 'que cet apôtre soit venu de France'.[23]

PLATE 8: Abbey of Saint-Benoît-du-Lac. Plate from *Propos d'un bâtisseur du Bon Dieu* (1949) showing cloister by Dom Bellot.

PLATE 9: Abbey of Saint-Benoît-du-Lac. Exterior of tower of Saint-Jean-Baptiste by Dom Bellot.

After giving his lectures in Canada, Dom Bellot returned to Wisques, but was back in Canada in 1936 in order to arrange his work on the completion of the dome of the Oratoire Saint-Joseph-du-Mont-Royal in Montreal which Père Bergeron had asked him to undertake. The Oratoire had been begun in 1915 to designs by J. Dalbé Viau and L. Alphonse Venne, and Bellot collaborated with Lucien Parent and René-Rodolphe Tourville on the design of a dome consisting of two concrete shells topped by a cupola (Plate 7). Furthermore, in 1935 Bellot had been invited to prepare a scheme for the abbey of Saint-Benoît-du-Lac, where his collaborators were Félix Racicot (1903–73) and Dom Claude-Marie Côté (1909–86). Work started on this in 1939. Based on a pentagonal plan, and incomplete when Bellot died, the initial stage of the abbey is built of reinforced concrete faced with stone, and has corner towers and a characteristic cloister and refectory with polychromatic brick arches and walls (Plates 8–10).[24]

PLATE 10: Abbey of Saint-Benoît-du-Lac. Plate from *Propos d'un bâtisseur du Bon Dieu* (1949) of exterior from south-east showing part of abbey by Dom Bellot.

Publication of the *Propos* (1949)

It was not until 1949, fifteen years after they were given and five years after Bellot's death, that the lectures were published in the book *Propos d'un bâtisseur du Bon Dieu*. Although in the last decade of his life Bellot had brought out some of them individually in journals, as well as publishing articles on related themes, he resisted making them more permanently public. When finally issued as a single volume, they took the form of a book with 128 pages of text, sixteen sepia photographs (a portrait of Bellot, and fifteen views of buildings), a preface by Père Henri-Paul Bergeron CSC (1911–87), and an introduction by Henri Charlier.

Bergeron, who also gave the volume his *Nihil obstat*, was a priest at the Oratoire Saint-Joseph in Montreal where Frère André has an honoured place; Bergeron was author of several books on him and on the Oratoire – including *Le Frère André, CSC, L'apôtre de Saint-Joseph* (1938, etc) and *L'Oratoire Saint-Joseph, œuvre du frère André* (1941, etc.) – and it was Bergeron who wrote Bellot's obituary in the journal *L'Oratoire* in 1945.[25] A man of culture and sensitivity, he played a major rôle in Bellot's work at the Oratoire.[26]

In his preface to the *Propos*, Bergeron explains that it was only at 'les instances de ses amis' that Bellot agreed to have his lectures published. In 1934, eight young architects and artists had subscribed $50 which they sent to Bellot, urging him to publish his lectures; they received a typed version of them by the middle of the next year, and fourteen years later this served as a basis for the *Propos*.[27] The publishers, Éditions Fides, were founded in Montreal in 1937 and have a close association with the Congrégation de Sainte-Croix who provide the priests for the Oratoire Saint-Joseph. Bergeron notes in his preface that the *Propos* was to be the first of three 'Cahiers d'Art ARCA' devoted to Bellot by Éditions Fides: the second was to consist of the presentation of Bellot's main works, and the third would reveal his discoveries in the realm of architectural proportion, under the title *Le secret de l'harmonie dans l'art*. The *Propos* was volume 4 in the 'Cahiers d'Art ARCA' series, the first three being Henri Charlier's *Peinture, sculpture, broderie et vitrail*, introduced by Maurice Brillant (1942), and the two volumes of Marius Barbeau's *Saintes artisanes* (1944, 1946).[28]

Charlier, in his introduction to the *Propos*, combines biography with an enthusiastic appraisal of Bellot's work, as he had done in his introductory essay in *Une œuvre d'architecture moderne* of 1927 and subsequently in articles on Bellot in *L'artisan liturgique*, *Liturgical Arts* and elsewhere.[29] Apart from providing sculpture in several European locations where Bellot worked – including Annecy, Solesmes, Troyes, Vanves and at La Pierre-qui-Vire – Charlier travelled to Canada and supplied the crucifixion, altar and the twelve apostles and other figures for the Oratoire Saint-Joseph in Montreal. At the abbey of Saint-Benoît-du-Lac, the statue of Saint Benedict in the tower of Saint-Benoît is by him. Despite his visits to Canada, however, Charlier kept his roots in France, where he was associated with the monastic community at Mesnil-Saint-Loup (Aube), between Sens and Troyes.[30]

The *Propos* consists essentially of the nine lectures which Bellot originally gave, presented in eight chapters,[31] with the fifteen photographs of buildings placed at the end of the volume. Rather than illustrating the lectures, these cover nine projects by Bellot referred to by Charlier in his introduction: four of these (Oosterhout, Quarr, Bloomendaal and Noordhoek) had already appeared in 1927 in *Une œuvre d'architecture moderne*; the remaining five, presented together for the first time, are Saint-Benoît-du-Lac and the Oratoire Saint-Joseph in Canada, and in France the Church of the Immaculate Conception at Audincourt (Doubs), the Church of Notre-Dame-des-Trévois at Troyes, and the Monastère des Tourelles at Montpellier. These three French buildings had been erected following Bellot's return to Wisques from Oosterhout in 1928, and demonstrate his experimentation with reinforced concrete.[32]

The range of Bellot's ideas in the *Propos* can be seen from the chapter headings: his concern for the use of brick and concrete, light and colour, his commitment to a system of proportions in building, and his belief in beauty in architecture as an expression of the divine as mediated by St Thomas Aquinas. Such concerns echo those given by Charlier in his introduction to *Une œuvre d'architecture moderne* of 1927. Throughout, Bellot emphasises the importance of historical evolution, in which the new in architecture must reflect a continuation of the old and not a complete rejection of it. In this context, Bellot commends Anatole de Baudot's church of Saint-Jean-de-Montmartre in Paris (1894–1904) with its exploration of the Cottancin form of construction using cement, concrete and brick. Bellot admires the courage and tenacity needed by Baudot to complete this remarkable building: Bellot's own combination of concrete and brick was never to match the audacity displayed by Baudot.[33]

Among writers whom Bellot quotes approvingly are the Catholic publisher and poet Charles Péguy (1873–1914), with his strong support of the uniqueness of creativity and his opposition to standardisation. In terms of architectural practice, Bellot cites the writings of four architects or architectural theorists in particular: Viollet-le-Duc, Desiderius Lenz, Odilo Wolff and Le Corbusier. But Bellot's overarching concern is with the relationship between beauty and the divine, and for an interpretation of St Thomas' writings he turns to the Catholic philosopher Maritain.

Maritain

Jacques Maritain (1882–1973) was a friend and confidant of artists, writers, poets and musicians, and is thought by many to have had the finest aesthetic sensibility among the major figures of twentieth-century European philosophy. Maritain's publications on almost every aspect of art began with his book *Art et scolastique* of 1920 and culminated in the publication of *Creative Intuition in Art and Poetry* in 1953 and *The Responsibility of the Artist* in 1960. Maritain, like Péguy, is quoted with approval by Bellot, who had met the philospher at Oosterhout; moreover we know that Maritain went to see the monks on the Isle of Wight in 1907,[34] and that in 1914 he and his wife Raïssa visited Quarr.[35]

In the *Propos*, Bellot turns to Maritain both as a Catholic philosopher committed to the arts and as the leading contemporary *Thomiste*. Time and again, Bellot says that a specifically religious (i.e. Catholic) architecture can only be produced by artists and architects who are themselves religious (i.e. Catholic). As the premises of *L'Arche* maintain, artists should collaborate in the creation of *l'art sacré*. To Bellot, *Thomisme* is

> une atmosphère où peuvent vivre et s'épanouir toutes les valeurs spirituelles;
> il est, par excellence, le climat des philosophes chrétiens, riche de tous les
> siècles passés et capable d'assimiler, en les ramenant à l'unité, toutes les parcelles
> de vérité. (*Propos* 58)

As the author of *Art et scolastique*, says Bellot, Maritain may be numbered among those 'jeunes philosophes' who have established a new aesthetic in which 'nous souhaitons une collaboration entre philosophes et artistes'; apart from *Art et scolastique*, adds Bellot, other recent publications which attempt to do this include *Le procès de l'art* by Stanislas Fumet (1929), *Les nouvelles théories sur l'art moderne* (1922) by Maurice Denis and, above all, the diverse articles by Henri Charlier. But it is Maritain's chapter on 'Art and beauty' in *Art et scolastique* which Bellot finds especially sympathetic.[36]

Bellot affirms St Thomas' statement that the essence of beauty lies in two points: 'il est *objet* de connaissance et objet tel qu'il *délecte la connaissance*' (*Propos* 60). Or, as St Thomas expresses it elsewhere, 'On appelle beau ce dont la vue nous plaît'. Following Plato, Aristotle and St Augustine, St Thomas regards order as essential to beauty. 'Le beau', says St Thomas, 'consiste dans une juste proportion des choses'. To Bellot, this phrase says it all (*Propos* 61–2).

Beauty, St Thomas continues, requires three conditions: integrity, clarity and proportion, all of which vary according to the requirements of different works of art. The practice of the artist has to be set within the science of aesthetics. Yet Bellot is almost apologetic about the demands he is making. 'Vous m'excuserez de vous avoir conduits dans les sentiers de la philosophie', he writes. 'Mais les hauteurs que nous venons de gravir, ne doivent pas vous être étrangères.' He then goes on:

> C'est là que peuvent se rejoindre et s'unifier, comme il convient, votre vie professionnelle et votre vie d'homme, intellectuelle et chrétienne. Votre œuvre émanera alors de tout vous-même, procédera de toutes les valeurs qui sont en vous, aura la plénitude et la vigueur requises pour être vraiment utile à la société.

Bellot ends with a flourish:

> Avec le beau, c'est l'être même, c'est le reflet de Dieu que nous atteignons; de ce Dieu, qui, naturellement et surnaturellement, est la fin de notre vie humaine; et notre esthétique doit inspirer la technique qui dirige immédiatement notre art. (*Propos* 65)

Thus, art which proceeds from our innermost spirits becomes creative and vital: 'Voilà le secret de l'art vivant, le ressort et le régulateur de progrès en architecture' (*Propos* 66). It was this which sustained the builders of Notre-Dame in Paris and the cathedrals at Chartres, Amiens and Beauvais, the Sainte-Chapelle, Mont-Saint-Michel and other masterpieces.

The influence of Maritain's interpretation of the writings of St Thomas on Bellot should not be seen in isolation, for Bellot's monastic training at Quarr would have been under Dom Paul Delatte osb (1848–1937), who was Abbot of Solesmes from 1890 to 1921. Dom Delatte held a doctorate in theology from the Institut Catholique de Lille, where he taught philosophy before becoming a monk.[37] Dom Jean Rochon osb, the present archivist at the abbey of Saint-Benoît-du-Lac, stresses the impact of a Thomist training on Bellot's architecture. 'On devine l'intérêt particulier que le frère Bellot, comme architecte, pouvait prendre à cet enseignement et les solides fondements qu'y trouverait bientôt son art', Père Rochon writes. He continues:

> Alors que la pratique de la prière liturgique l'éclairait sur l'aménagement des lieux, la fréquentation de la Bible lui faisait comprendre leur profond symbolisme et la métaphysique thomiste l'initiait aux notions les plus hautes, en même temps que les plus fonctionnelles pour l'art les plus satisfaisantes pour l'esprit, sur les aspects fondamentaux de l'être que sont le beau, le vrai et le bien.[38]

It was, then, Aquinas who provided a firm theological base for Bellot's architectural practice and writings. In order to give a sharper focus, Bellot refers in the *Propos* to the publications of Viollet-le-Duc, Desiderius Lenz, Odilo Wolff and Le Corbusier. Let us look more closely at Bellot's comments on them.

Viollet-le-Duc

It is hardly surprising that the architect, scholar and restorer Eugène-Emmanuel Viollet-le-Duc (1814–79) features so prominently in the *Propos*, for Dom Bellot acknowledges his admiration for him elsewhere. Thus we find Bellot in 1931 writing as follows in his autobiography:

> Avec la formation architecturale donnée par mon père et augmentée de celle de l'Ecole des Beaux-Arts, c'est VIOLLET-LE-DUC qui m'a le plus influencé. Il m'a fait comprendre la logique et la sincérité de cette architecture française du Moyen-Age improprement appelée gothique. Lorsque j'ai passé mon examen de diplôme, je connaissais sur le bout du doigt le dictionnaire du grand restaurateur de nos églises.

Bellot next becomes more specific:

> Avec lui j'ai appris à méditer l'archéologie; et j'ai vu que faire de l'architecture romane ou gothique sans en avoir compris l'esprit et dégagé les principes, copier des ornements gothiques dans des conditions différentes de celles où se trouvaient les constructeurs du Moyen-Age ce n'est plus faire de l'architecture, mais un simple travail manuel.

Bellot had also found Choisy in his *Histoire d'architecture* a liberating influence: 'Il met parfaitement en relief l'âme de toutes ces époques,' he writes of Choisy, 'montre l'habilité des constructeurs, et dégage de toutes les compositions l'essentiel sans s'arrêter aux détails ou à l'accidentel'.[39]

But Bellot bypasses Choisy in the *Propos* and turns instead to Viollet-le-Duc, whose *Dictionnaire raisonné de l'architecture française du XIe au XVIe siècle* had been published in Paris in ten volumes between 1854 and 1868.[40] The *Dictionnaire* is arranged alphabetically and extends from small details (e.g. 'gousset') to broad conceptual topics (e.g. 'construction'), and in his lectures Bellot quotes from three of the wider subjects covered by Viollet-le-Duc – namely taste, style and proportion. Let us look at these more closely.[41]

Taste

Dom Bellot deals with taste in Lecture 1 on *Le renouveau de l'art et du goût* (*Propos* 27–40).[42] To Bellot, there is good taste which discerns what is truly beautiful, and bad taste which does not. But there is a deeper dimension, he says, for 'un goût de travers est en somme un défaut d'esprit'. As Viollet-le-Duc makes clear, taste cannot be separated from truth and morality:

> Le goût est l'habitude du beau et du bien; pour être un homme de goût, il est donc essentiel de discerner le bien du mal, le beau du laid. Le goût . . . est encore le respect pour le vrai. (*Dictionnaire*, tome 6, p. 31; *Propos* 38)

Bellot endorses Viollet-le-Duc's identification of the struggle, in the words of T. S. Eliot, between 'tradition and the individual talent'.[43] 'On a pensé, depuis longtemps déjà', writes Viollet-le-Duc, qu'il suffisait pour faire preuve de goût, d'adopter certains types reconnus beaux, et de ne jamais s'en écarter. Cette méthode, admise par l'Académie des Beaux-Arts en ce qui touche l'architecture, nous a conduit à prendre pour l'expression du goût certaines formules banales, à exclure la variété, l'invention, et à mettre hors la loi du goût tous les artistes qui cherchaient à exprimer des besoins nouveaux par des formes nouvelles, ou tout au moins soumises à de nouvelles applications. (*Dictionnaire*, tome 6, p. 32; *Propos* 39)

Thus the Académie des Beaux-Arts forces its members to submit to formulae whose meaning is never explained, and architectural taste, instead of being derived from a true and general principle, has become the prerogative of an exclusive school. Taste in architecture, says Viollet-le-Duc, must depend on more than just acceptance of a received style:

Toute forme d'architecture qui ne peut être donnée comme la conséquence d'une idée, d'un besoin, d'une nécessité, ne peut être regardée comme une œuvre de goût. (*Dictionnaire*, tome 6, p. 33; *Propos* 41)

Difficult though it may be, taste can be acquired. As Viollet-le-Duc puts it:

Le goût n'est pas, comme le pensent quelques-uns, une fantaisie plus ou moins heureuse, le résultat d'un instinct. Personne ne naît homme de goût. Le goût, au contraire, n'est que l'empreinte laissée par une éducation bien dirigée, le couronnement d'un labeur patient, le reflet du milieu dans lequel on vit. Savoir ne voir que de belles choses, s'en nourrir, comparer, arriver par la comparaison à choisir, se défier des jugements tout faits, chercher à discerner le vrai du faux, fuir la médiocrité, craindre l'engouement; c'est le moyen de former son goût. (*Dictionnaire*, tome 6, p. 34; *Propos* 42)

Viollet-le-Duc's writings deserve closer acquaintance, says Bellot. At the end of the day, in Bellot's view, 'l'art vrai éduque le goût; la corruption de l'art entraîne celle du goût; la dépravation du goût est la cause de l'anarchie des arts sous toutes ses formes' (*Propos* 42).

Bellot remains ambiguous about Viollet-le-Duc as a practising architect. Unfortunately, he writes, Viollet 'ne présentait pas d'exemple à l'appui de ses paroles, celles-ci, tombant sur un terrain mal préparé, ne trouvèrent que peu ou pas d'écho'. For himself, Bellot in the *Propos* denounces his own education at the École des Beaux-Arts: 'Je sais par expérience cette tyrannie qui peut résulter d'une trop grande habitude de l'architecture classique'. Up to the year 1900, students were taught how to design plans, 'mais on nous abandonnait, pour les formes, à une routine désespérante' (*Propos* 42-3).

Happily, since leaving the École, Bellot had found artistic satisfaction within the Benedictine community:

L'apprentissage de la vie monastique, fort heureusement, me permit de me livrer vraiment à la réflexion, de me dégager de la fascination des formes anciennes et de découvrir, pour mon profit, l'âme même de la tradition, son courant vital, et, en lui, les principes perdurables de l'art et du goût. (*Propos* 43)

That said, Bellot had to admit to his Canadian audience that the USA had benefited in terms of architecture and architectural education from architects trained in Paris at the École des Beaux-Arts.[44]

Style

Next, in Lecture 2 on *Les conditions d'un vrai style*, Dom Bellot draws a distinction between 'styles' and 'style' from the entry on style in Viollet-le-Duc's *Dictionnaire raisonné de l'architecture française*.[45]

'Les styles', says Bellot, following Viollet-le-Duc, 'sont des types de formes. Ce sont les caractères dont l'ensemble fait distinguer entre elles les époques et les écoles'; 'le style', on the other hand, 'est la manière d'être, disons le mode qui appartient à l'œuvre d'art en général, en tant qu'elle est une conception de l'esprit humain' (*Propos* 46–7). Again, there is a distinction between *le style absolu* which is 'la manifestation d'un idéal établi sur un principe', and *le style relatif* which 'se modifie selon l'objet, il est commandé à l'intelligence par la destination de l'œuvre' (*Propos* 48). By this last token, a style suitable for a church would not be suitable for a house.

Bellot then stresses that in building it is necessary to submit to 'toutes sortes de disciplines, celles de l'âme, celles de l'intelligence en particulier, celles enfin que les matériaux employés nous imposent' (*Propos* 48). Regrettably, most of his contemporaries want to be free of all constraints, whereas to Bellot himself freedom depends on rules:

> Ce sont ces lois qui nous libèrent, ces contraintes qui nous guident, ces disciplines qui nous affranchissent et nous permettent de donner à nos talents leur maximum de rendement. Lorsqu'un groupe bien uni saura se soumettre à des lois, alors nous verrons poindre l'aurore d'une architecture nouvelle, d'un style nouveau, qui sera vraiment du 'style'. (*Propos* 49)

Dom Bellot cites the collaboration at Wisques of artists from the Netherlands, Belgium and France as an example of such an approach, and he urges Canadians to follow this example.

Proportion

Dom Bellot makes clear at the start of Chapter 6 on *Oeuvre d'art et technique – Les proportions* that proportion is a key feature of his architecture:

> La technique que, pour ma part, j'ai essayé d'adopter comme conforme aux justes exigences, non seulement de l'art bien compris mais encore de l'art chrétien, je veux dire la technique intellectuelle qui met la forme au principe de toute réalisation artistique . . . cette technique fait jouer un rôle fondamental aux proportions. (*Propos* 101)

After giving his reasons for this, and drawing a distinction between symmetry and proportion, Bellot turns to Viollet-le-Duc for support, and quotes from the entry on proportion in his *Dictionnaire raisonné de l'architecture française*, lest it be thought that 'tout cela, loi, science de proportion, nuit à l'inspiration me dira-t-on' (*Propos* 104–5).[46] As Viollet-le-Duc puts it:

> Un système géométrique ou arithmétique, propre à établir des lois de proportions, loin d'être une entrave est au contraire un auxiliaire indispensable; car il faut bien nous servir du T, et de l'équerre, et du compas pour exprimer nos idées. Nous ne pouvons établir un édifice à l'aide d'un empirisme vague,

indéfini. Disons-le aussi, jamais les règles dans la production de l'esprit humain, n'ont été une entrave que pour les médiocrités ignorantes; elles sont un secours efficace et un stimulant pour les esprits d'élite. (*Dictionnaire*, tome 7, p. 550; *Propos* 105)

Music provides an example. 'Les règles si sévères de l'harmonie musicale ont-elles étouffé l'inspiration des artistes?', Viollet-le-Duc asks. 'Il en est de même pour la construction', he continues, particularly in the Middle Ages:

Le mérite des bâtisseurs du Moyen-Age a été de posséder des règles bien définies; et de s'y soumettre, et de s'en servir. Un malheur aujourd'hui dans les arts, et particulièrement dans l'architecture, c'est de croire qu'l'on peut faire œuvre de valeur sous l'inspiration de la pure fantaisie; et que l'on puisse élever un monument avec cette donnée très vague que l'on peut appeler 'le goût', comme on compose une toilette de femme. (*Dictionnaire*, tome 7, p. 550; *Propos* 105)

In the Middle Ages, they knew better:

Nos maîtres du Moyen-Age étaient plus sérieux, et quand ils posaient la règle et l'équerre sur une tablette, ils savaient comment ils allaient procéder; ils marchaient méthodiquement, sans passer leur temps à crayonner au hasard, en attendant cette inspiration vague, à laquelle les esprits paresseux s'habituent à rendre un culte. (*Dictionnaire*, tome 7, p. 550; *Propos* 105)

Bellot ends his section on Viollet-le-Duc's views on proportion (and how they coincide with his own) with a peroration. 'Vous, les bâtisseurs, qui êtes tous des gens sérieux,' he writes, 'vous devez comprendre mieux que personne la nécessité d'une discipline esthétique dans vos constructions' (*Propos* 105).

Dom Bellot then moves on in the *Propos* to a historical consideration of proportion in architecture from Pythagoras to Viollet-le-Duc and beyond. However, Bellot admits that, although he had often read the passage on proportions in Viollet's *Dictionnaire*, it had left him rather indifferent: 'ses schémas m'avaient laissé un peu inerte', as he put it (*Propos* 109). Luckily for Bellot, inspiration was at hand.

Lenz and Wolff

This came when he heard of the German Benedictine abbey at Beuron, and the work there of Dom Desiderius Lenz osb (1832–1928). Lenz, a sculptor and architect, had founded the Beuron art school in 1894 with the purpose of renewing sacred art, and he and others had carried out extensive rebuilding and decoration at Beuron, at the abbey of Monte Cassino, and elsewhere.[47] Bellot was excited by his discovery.

As Bellot explains, the system of proportion which he advocates in the *Propos* is 'd'une souplesse incomparable, beaucoup plus riche en combinaisons que tous ceux que j'ai étudiés'. But he is under no illusion as to the difficulty of using such a system:

Il faut des années de réflexion et de recherches. C'est par la patience que l'on possède son âme et son art. Je dois vous dire d'abord que le grand confort n'est pas l'apanage des moines. Pendant vingt-six ans, j'ai vécu comme un ermite, ne recevant aucune revue. Ne croyez donc pas qu'il faille courir le monde, et aller voir des quantités de gens très forts, pour faire des progrès. (*Propos* 109)

With few means at his disposal, Bellot reflected on what he could possibly do to give his work real value.

One day, Bellot notes, he was sent pictures of Beuron, and a little later was given a small manual dealing with Dom Lenz's theories of geometry in religious art: in all likelihood this would have been a copy of Lenz's book *Zur Ästhetik der Beuroner Schule*, first published in German in 1898 (2nd edn 1927) and in a French translation as *L'esthétique de Beuron* in 1905.[48] It was a revelation. Here was that mysterious golden section, a magic wand which could transform commonplace art into a masterpiece: 'une certaine coupe d'or mystérieuse, vraie fée qui changeait l'art banal en chef-d'œuvre' (*Propos* 109).

Then suddenly, at Quarr Abbey, Bellot observes, there appeared a copy of Père Odilo Wolff's book *Tempelmasse. Das Gesetz der Proportion in den antiken und altchristlichen Sakralbauten. Ein Beitrag zur Kunstwissenschaft und Ästhetik*, which had been published in Vienna in 1912.[49] According to Wolff, the hexagon and 60-degree triangle had governed the whole of ancient art, and he provides analytical diagrams to support his case (Plate 11). As Bellot was at this time designing Quarr, it is 'entièrement faite avec le triangle à 60-degrès, que j'avais soumis à une gymnastique acrobatique, pour trouver toutes les proportions de cette grande église, la première que je construisais' (*Propos* 109–10).[50]

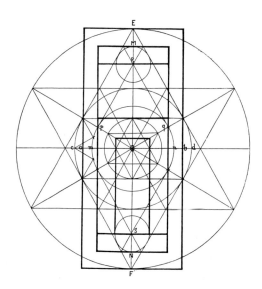

PLATE 11: The Parthenon, Athens, from Odilo Wolff, *Tempelmasse . . .* (1912), plate 19.

There is little doubt that Bellot was committed practically to the use of the golden section as well as the hexagon: indeed, he had a set-square made which would provide him with the proportions of the golden section. Elsewhere in the *Propos* he deals with the sacredness of numbers, observing that Pythagoras 'plaçait le bonheur suprême dans la contemplation de l'harmonie des Rythmes de l'Univers', and cites as his authority the writings of Matila Ghyka (*Propos* 106).[51] Bellot's expression of his hopes to write more extensively on proportion fits in with Père Bergeron's remark in his Preface to the *Propos* that a projected volume by Dom Bellot in the Cahiers d'Art ARCA series was to be entitled *Le secret de l'harmonie dans l'art* (*Propos* 10).

Le Corbusier

The Swiss-born architect Charles-Edouard Jeanneret, known as Le Corbusier (1887–1966), whose interest in numbers and proportional systems is well known, was also fascinated by the golden section and by Matila Ghyka's writings on it: his *tracés régulateurs*, for instance, represent a significant aspect of his thinking. But this is an aspect of Le Corbusier's work which is virtually ignored by Dom Bellot, whose comments on Le Corbusier in his writings are almost entirely negative.

Although there are few direct references in the *Propos* to Le Corbusier by name, his spirit is frequently invoked by Bellot as representing the moral poverty of artists outside Catholicism. Bellot presents Le Corbusier in Chapter 1 on *Le renouveau de l'art et du goût* as typifying the nihilism and aridity of the work of some contemporary architects: 'L'art avait fait table rase du passé et prétendait créer un homme nouveau, mais cet homme nouveau n'a été qu'une caricature' (*Propos* 28). Bellot then points out that 'un Suisse, nommé Le Corbusier, s'est installé grand pontife de cette conjuration contre la tradition'. The book *Le cheval de Troie du Bolchevisme*, says Bellot, 'démasque énergiquement les tendances' (*Propos* 30). In choosing this book, which came out in Bienne in 1931, Bellot was taking a polemical anti-Le Corbusier publication to suit his purposes.

The author of *Le cheval de Troie du Bolchevisme* was the Swiss architect and critic Alexander von Senger (1880–1968), also known as Alexandre de Senger, who had published a series of articles attacking Le Corbusier in the newspaper *La Suisse libérale*, published in Neuchâtel. Specifically, these pieces had taken as their point of departure the competition scheme for the Palace of the League of Nations in Geneva submitted in 1927 by Le Corbusier and his cousin, Pierre Jeanneret (1896–1967). These attacks were instrumental in ensuring the rejection of the Le Corbusier–Jeanneret scheme, and were brought together in book form as *Le cheval de Troie du Bolchevisme*. The Trojan horse in the title was none other than Le Corbusier himself.[52] Senger's aim (also expressed in his books *Krisis der Architektur* of 1928, and *Die Brandfackel Moskaus* of 1931) was to show that progressive architecture and its adherents were politically subversive, conspiratorial, pro-Jewish, Bolshevik, and committed to an inhuman architecture which challenged the values of the state.[53]

Bellot begins by acknowledging the Swiss architect's belief in the educational value of art but rejects 'la doctrine dont Le Corbusier est l'apôtre' of which the leitmotif is 'mort à la tradition' (*Propos* 30). Le Corbusier, in his commitment to the machine aesthetic, has lost much. To Bellot, the vision behind all great architecture inspires something akin to radiance in a cultured man and sharpens his taste for life. Here, Le Corbusier fails:

> Les œuvres de Le Corbusier provoquent des sentiments contraires; on frissonne, le sens vital se relâche (une dame nommait une de ces maisons: une caisse à suicide), l'on ressent un vide intérieur, une sorte d'angoisse, comme si l'on plongeait les regards dans un cratère éteint de la lune. (*Propos* 31)

These views have a political and national dimension. For, says Bellot, they have been promoted by the international journal *L'Esprit Nouveau*, a nihilistic enterprise with vaguely international aims, the majority of whose contributors do not have French names.

L'Esprit Nouveau, of course, had been founded in 1920 by Le Corbusier, Amédée Ozenfant and Paul Dermée as an international review of aesthetics. Many of the ideas in Le Corbusier's early books were first put forward in articles for *L'Esprit Nouveau*, and the Pavillon de l'Esprit Nouveau at the 1925 Paris Exposition had given it wider publicity. Time and again, Bellot expresses his opposition to it. He opposes 'architectes bolchevistes militants' producing 'petites boîtes à habiter' (*Propos* 32). Sun, air and hygiene are all important, it is true. But, asks Bellot,

> que faites-vous de l'hygiène du cœur, de l'esprit, de l'âme? Nous nous inscrivons contre ces produits stériles et faux de l'art soi-disant moderne, vides de tout contenu spirituel et humain, et exerçant leur action chez l'homme normal et sain. (*Propos* 33)

To Bellot, the aspirations of the artist must lead to God:

> Qu'il soit littérateur, musicien, peintre, sculpteur ou architecte, s'il ne méconnaît pas le sens de sa vocation, l'artiste doit s'adresser à l'âme de l'homme pour le conduire et le maintenir sur les sommets où l'on rencontre Dieu. (*Propos* 33)

In contrast to the inhumanity propounded by Le Corbusier and his followers, says Bellot,

> l'œuvre d'architecture doit être évocatrice de joie par la lumière, de recueillement par l'ombre, de repos par le silence; ainsi elle est vraiment humaine. Elle atteint ce but par le jeu de volumes, d'espace et de lignes qui, renvoyant de la lumière à l'ombre, de l'ombre à la lumière, équilibrent nos perceptions en les prolongeant. (*Propos* 34)

The Church, claims Bellot, in opposition to the views of Le Corbusier and *L'Esprit Nouveau*, has always been a protector of the arts and been anxious not to let any of these human values disappear.[54]

Bellotisme and Bellotistes

The reception of the *Propos* was muted, and in Canada only religious periodicals seem to have acknowledged its publication. But at least their comments were favourable, both personally and professionally. Thus Jacques Tremblay in the

Jesuit magazine *Relations*, after summarising its contents, describes it as the work of 'le Bénédictin génial que fut Dom Bellot';[55] to André Tilly in *La revue dominicaine*, the book 'nous oblige à réfléchir, à reviser nos opinions sur l'art';[56] the reviewer in *Les carnets Viatoriens* (published by the Clercs de Saint-Viateur) writes that the pages of the *Propos* 'précisent certaines données fondamentales sur l'art et sur la métaphysique du beau; elles éclairent l'intelligence et développent le goût de tout lecteur sincère';[57] and Victor Barbeau in the journal *Liaison*, published in Montreal, observes that Bellot's interior of the monastery of Saint-Benoît-du-Lac, particularly the cloister, 'est la plus belle œuvre d'art dont il a doté notre pays'.[58]

PLATE 12: Sherbrooke, Quebec. Crypt of Seminary of Saint-Charles-Borromée, by Edgar Courchesne.

Although both Père Bergeron in his Preface to the *Propos*, and Charlier in his introduction to it, make clear that Bellot was reluctant to publish his lectures,[59] Bellot did bring out several in periodicals as well as publishing supplementary essays which promoted his ideas and those of his supporters.[60] However, the periodical *L'art sacré*, published in Paris from 1935 and promoting functionalist ideas in religious art and architecture, was available in Canada. Led by

PLATE 13: Abbey of Saint-Benoît-du-Lac. Exterior showing (from left) tower of Saint-Jean-Baptiste by Dom Bellot, church by Dan Hanganu, and hospice and campanile by Dom Côté.

Dominicans Marie-Alain Couturier (1877–1954) and Pie-Raymond Régamey (1900–96) this opposed Bellot and his followers. Nonetheless Bellotisme was supported by architects such as Dufresne and Courchesne, whose friendship with Bellot went back to the 1920s and whose ecclesiastical buildings were strongly influenced by him: a striking example is Courchesne's crypt in the seminary of Saint-Charles-Borromée in Sherbooke, Quebec (Plate 12).[61] On Bellot's death in 1944, his work at Saint-Benoît-du-Lac was continued by Dom Côté, who added the hostel, campanile and further cloisters,[62] and in 1994 the abbey was completed with the addition of the church, designed by the Canadian architect Dan Hanganu in a style which reflects some of Bellot's ideas (Plate 13).

Unfortunately, Bellot's hopes of starting in Canada a similar body to *L'Arche* were disappointed, and he had no qualms in disowning some architects who failed to understand his work and ideas. Regrettably, says Bergeron, Bellot had to suffer 'les attaques de certains rivaux jaloux et impuissants' (*Propos* 10), and all told, comments Charlier, Bellot, a true Parisian, suffered greatly in exile, forced to live in Canada 'avec des hommes n'ayant pas la moindre idée des préoccupations intellectuelles d'un artiste' (*Propos* 23).

Since Dom Bellot's death in 1944, little apart from the *Propos* has been published about him, and whereas present-day Benedictine communities readily acknowledge his work, only in Canada were there formal expressions to mark the fiftieth anniversary of his death in 1994.[63] In England, the pioneer apologist for Bellot was the religious writer Peter Anson (1889–1975); in 1944 he published an article on Bellot in the Benedictine magazine *Pax* which was reprinted in the New York journal *Liturgical Arts* in the following year.[64] In 1967, Sir Nikolaus Pevsner brought out a perceptive article on Quarr Abbey in *The Architectural Review* which pointed to Bellot's significance as an expressionist architect, influenced by Catalonian gothic.[65] But despite Pevsner's urging, this led to no extensive study of Bellot's buildings or writings. Unlike the Dutch Benedictine Hans van der Laan (1904–91), who had met Bellot at Oosterhout, and whose architectural theories and abbey at Vaals have benefited from the research and publications of Richard Padovan, Bellot's buildings and writings have been neglected.[66] A reappraisal is long overdue.

NOTES

1. Among the major documentary sources for Dom Bellot are the archives at the abbeys at Wisques and Saint-Benoît-du-Lac, and at the Oratoire Saint-Joseph in Montreal. For help in these locations I am grateful to Christian Decotignie and Dom Michel Hecquet OSB (Wisques), Dom Jean Rochon OSB (Saint-Benoît-du-Lac), and Fr Marcel Lalonde CSC and Fr Bernard LaFrenière CSC (Oratoire Saint-Joseph). At Quarr Abbey, I benefited from the assistance of Dom Charles Fitzsimons OSB, and at Solesmes from Dom Louis Soltner OSB.

2. These and other biographical details are from Bellot's folder for the École des Beaux-Arts in the Archives Nationales, Paris, AJ/52/400, and from personal communication with the late Peter Burton, whose unpublished thesis of 1975 on Bellot's building of Quarr is kept at the abbey. Dom Bellot's mother's name was Marie Antoinette Émilie (*née* Charlot).

3. For an early study of Dom Paul Bellot's work in a wide context, see Dom Eugène Roulin, *Nos Églises. Liturgie, architecture moderne et contemporaine, mobilier, peinture et sculpture* (Paris: P. Lethielleux, 1938), published in an English translation by C. Cornelia Craigie and John A. Southwell as *Modern Church Architecture* (St Louis MO: B. Herder Book Company, 1947). Dom Roulin (1860–1939) was a monk of Solesmes who moved to Ampleforth Abbey in 1905, and Peter Howell alerted me to his writings. More recently, see Nicole Tardif-Painchaud, *Dom Bellot et l'architecture religieuse au Québec* (Quebec: Les Presses de l'université Laval, 1978); Claude Bergeron, *L'architecture des églises du Québec* (Quebec: Les Presses de l'université Laval, 1987); and Jean Rochon, 'L'esprit d'un moine bâtisseur. Dom Paul Bellot (1876–1944)', *Chercher Dieu*, no. 16 (Spring 1994), 10–39. See also the six articles on Bellot by Dom Guy-Marie Oury OSB, published in the magazine *L'ami de Saint-Benoît-du-Lac* between 1987 and 1992 (nos 71–4, 78, 80).

4. Bellot's *Feuille de Valeurs* (or record of marks) documents his period of study at the École, and to Richard Chafee it shows that 'as a student Bellot was able and persevering but not outstanding' (letter to Peter Willis from the late Peter Burton, 17 January 1992). See Richard Chafee, 'The teaching of architecture at the École des Beaux-Arts', in Arthur Drexler (ed.), *The Architecture of the École des Beaux-Arts* (London: Secker and Warburg, 1977), pp. 61–109.

5. Bellot's final diploma design was published in *L'architecture au salon 1901* (Paris: Armand Guérinet, 1901), plates 6–8. It is listed as no. 3,714 in *Explication des ouvrages de peinture, sculpture, architecture, gravure et lithographie des artistes vivants exposés au Grand Palais des Beaux-Arts* (Paris: Paul Dupont, 1901). Bellot's entry no. 3,715 is described as *La vieille cathédrale de Salamanque (Espagne)*. In the 1902 edition of the same catalogue, Bellot's entry no. 3,061 is called a *Projet pour la reconstruction de l'église Saint-Germain, à Flers (Orne)*. The catalogue for the 1898 Salon, incidentally, records two drawings by Bellot (nos 4,264–5) entitled *Souvenir de Londres*. The copies of these catalogues which I used were in the library of the Musée d'Orsay in Paris.

6. The text and plates are in a box, and, according to the reviewers in *The New York Herald Tribune* (Books Section, Sunday 22 May 1927, p. 10) and *The Catholic World* (March 1928, pp. 850–2), the English edition cost $50, though the reviewer in *The Commonweal* (30 March 1927, pp. 584–5) prices it at $25.

7. Père Fabre considered *L'Arche* in his book *Pages d'art chrétien. Etudes d'architecture, de peinture, de sculpture et d'iconographie* (Paris: Maison de la Bonne Presse, 1920;

2nd edn 1926). See also his article 'L'Arche', *La vie et les arts liturgiques*, vol. 4, no. 48 (December 1918), 616–19, which followed the anonymous essay (apparently by Maurice Storez) entitled 'Ce qu'est l'Arche. Un groupement de travail', *La vie et les arts liturgiques*, vol. 4, no. 46 (October 1918), 514–26. This includes a section on architecture on pp. 518–21 listing a ten-point 'credo' which Storez republished as 'Quelques principes d'architectures', *L'artisan liturgique*, vol. 3, no. 13 (April–June 1929), 246–7. It was illustrated with photographs of Bellot's work at Noordhoek, Heerlen and Bloemendaal. Another French follower of Bellot was James Bouillé (1894–1945), and Bellot wrote an article about his work, namely 'L'architecte James Bouillé', *L'artisan liturgique*, vol. 13, no. 55 (October–December 1939), 1,202–3.

8. *L'artisan liturgique*, vol. 3, no. 13 (April–June 1929) and vol. 7, no. 29 (April–June 1933).

9. B. J. Koldewey, 'Het Werk van Père Bellot', *Het Roomsh Katholiek Bouwblad*, year 1, no. 1 (14 August 1929), 5–8; year 1, no. 2 (29 August 1929), 14–7; year 1, no. 5 (10 October 1929), 57–60. For comments by Bellot, and a reply by Koldewey, see year 2, no. 10 (18 December 1930), 192. In 1935, Bellot published an article about his Dutch collaborator, Henk Charles van de Leur (1898–1994). See 'Eglises de Groningue et de Bolsward (Hollande). H. C. van de Leur, architecte', *L'architecture* (Paris), vol. 48, no. 5 (May 1935), 171–80.

10. *The Catholic World*, March 1928, pp. 850–2 (852).

11. *The New York Herald Tribune*, Books Section, Sunday 22 May 1927, p. 10.

12. *The Commonweal*, 30 March 1927, pp. 584–5 (585).

13. Extracts from these appear on p. 204. *La vraie France* contains essays on Psichari, Péguy, Bloy, Claudel, Mauriac, Maritain, Pétain, Copeau, Ghéon and Bellot. The Bellot text is on pp. 182–204 and is illustrated with a portrait of him by Père Marcel Plamondon CSC, which was reproduced again by Père Jean Rochon in his essay on Bellot in *Chercher Dieu*, no. 16 (Spring 1994), 10.

14. See note 29 below.

15. Notably through the publication of Fabre's *Pages d'art chrétien* in 1920 and the articles on Bellot in the journal *L'artisan liturgique*, which was started in 1927 by the Benedictine monks of the abbey of Saint-André in Bruges. Père Rochon has emphasised to me the rôle of Gérard Morisset (1898–1970) in promoting Bellot in Canada. See, for example, Morisset's articles 'Propos d'architecture. Le "classicisme" et ses faux dogmes', *Almanach de l'action sociale catholique*, vol. 12 (1928), 57–62; and 'Propos d'architecture. Architecture religieuse moderne', *Almanach de l'action sociale catholique*, vol. 13 (1929), 53–7.

16. See, for example, Edgar Courchesne, 'Un "poète de la brique"', *Le Devoir*, 13 December 1932; idem, 'Une œuvre d'architecture. Dom Paul Bellot, OSB, architecte', *Almanach de l'action sociale catholique*, vol. 17 (1933), 82–5; and idem, 'Dom Paul Bellot, OSB. Architecte ADGF', *The Journal, Royal Architectural Institute of Canada*, vol. 11, no. 2 (February 1934), 29–30. For his part, Dom Claude-Marie Côté OSB, Bellot's future collaborator at Saint-Benoît-du-Lac, also announced Bellot's forthcoming visit to Canada in 'Architecture religieuse et monastique', *Le Soleil*, 17 December 1932, which consists of a review of the Bellot exhibition of 1932. For Bellot's reception in Canada, see especially Tardif-Painchaud, *Dom Bellot*, pp. 47–61; Bergeron, *L'architecture des églises du Québec*, pp. 35–61; idem, *Architectures du XXe siècle au Québec, 1940–1985*

(Montreal: Musée de la Civilisation de Québec/Editions Méridien, 1989), pp. 117–26; and Harold Kalman, *A History of Canadian Architecture* (Toronto, New York and Oxford: Oxford University Press, 1994), vol. 2, pp. 729–32. See also the essay 'Dom Bellot au Canada', by Claude Bergeron and Nicole Tardif-Painchaud (forthcoming).

17. Père Henri-Paul Bergeron wrote to Solesmes, and Dom Georges Bellot forwarded the letter to his brother Dom Paul Bellot at Wisques on 15 October 1935. Claude Bergeron (no relation of Père Bergeron) tells me that this correspondence is in the Wisques MSS.

18. The admission tickets for the Montreal lectures described Bellot as 'Architecte diplômé par le Gouvernement Français / Grande médaille d'or de la Société Centrale des Architectes en 1932'.

19. The Wisques MSS contain typed copies of the text, with annotations, together with duplicated copies of the lectures for distribution. Christian Decotignie, who has studied these in detail, tells me that the original versions were amended before publication. Also at Wisques, there is an extensive collection of glass black-and-white slides which must have been used to illustrate the lectures, as many are labelled 'EDGAR GARIÉPY, PHOTOGRAPHE / PROJECTIONS, CINÉMA / 3635 HENRI-JULIEN, MONTRÉAL'.

20. For instance, *La Presse* on 12 February 1934 carried a prominent article on Bellot and a photograph of him with Maillard and Courchesne entitled 'Un éminent moine-architecte parmi nous'.

21. *Le Devoir*, 12 February 1934.

22. *La Presse*, 12 March 1934.

23. *Le Petit Journal*, 4 March 1934. However, Professor Geoffrey Simmins writes: 'It is a moot point . . . whether the Quebec audiences really understood the subtlety of Bellot's arguments. Bellot's lectures are so quintessentially French that it is difficult to understand them without some knowledge of the rich body of intellectual traditions they refer to – traditions going back to the Middle Ages. Although these ideas might have been shared by advanced French religious and artistic reformers, they quite probably seemed exotic and abstruse to Canadian listeners and readers'. Geoffrey Simmins (ed.), *Documents in Canadian Architecture* (Peterborough ON: Broadview Press, 1992), p. 173.

24. See Kalman, *A History of Canadian Architecture*, vol. 2, pp. 729–32.

25. Henri-Paul Bergeron, 'Un grand maître est passé parmi nous', *L'Oratoire*, vol. 34, no. 1 (January 1945), 18–19.

26. For Bergeron, see Étienne Catta, *Le Frère André (1845–1937) et l'Oratoire Saint-Joseph du Mont-Royal* (Montreal: Éditions Fides, 1965). As Catta records on p. 938, the memorial to Frère André at the Oratoire was designed by Bellot with a fresco by Charlier. Obituaries of Bergeron are in *L'Oratoire*, vol. 77, no. 2 (March 1988), 15, and *Cahiers de Joséphologie*, vol. 36, no. 2 (July–December 1988), 270. Père Jean Rochon brought these to my notice. The *Imprimatur* to the *Propos* was given by Père Albert Valois, *Vicaire Général*.

27. Claude Bergeron informed me of this.

28. These are listed in Jean-Rémi Brault, *Bibliographie des Éditions Fides, 1937–1987* (Montreal: Éditions Fides, 1987), pp. 269, 17, 29.

29. Articles by Charlier dealing with Bellot's work include (in chronological order) 'Architecture', *L'artisan liturgique*, vol. 3, no. 13 (April–June 1929), 243–5; 'L'art est une parabole', *L'artisan liturgique* vol. 7, no. 29 (April–June 1933), 596–7; 'The work of Dom Paul Bellot: Bellot: novelty and tradition', *Liturgical Arts*, vol. 4, no. 4 (1935), 134–47; 'Propos d'architecture', *Echanges et recherches*, vol. 2, no. 6 (April 1939), 378–83; 'L'art et l'intelligence' and 'L'art chrétien et les problèmes de l'art', *L'artisan liturgique*, vol. 14, no. 57 (April–June 1940), 1,236–45, 1,247–53; 'Dom Paul Bellot. Moine Bénédictin et architecte', *Compagnonnage*, vol. 5, no. 48 (February 1945), 3–4, 7; 'Dom Paul Bellot', *L'artisan liturgique*, vol. 15, no. 83 (October–December 1946) 57–74; and 'Dom Bellot', *Itinéraires*, no. 179 (January 1974), 21–40.

30. There is no full-scale biography of Charlier. For the context of Charlier's work see, for example, chapter 2 on 'La sculpture d'art moderne d'église' in Chanoine G. Arnaud d'Agnel, *L'art religieux moderne* (Grenoble: B. Arthaud, 1936), pp. 97–134. More recently, there is *Henri Charlier, statuaire et peintre* (Jarzé: Dominique Martin Morin, 1976) and *L'art sacré au XXe siècle en France*, Exhibition catalogue, Musée Municipal et Centre Culturel, Boulogne-Billancourt (1993), pp. 110–11. I am grateful to Père Jean Rochon and Dr Patrick Elliott, respectively, for alerting me to these two publications. Charlier's own books include *Le martyre de l'art, ou l'art livré aux bêtes. Suivi d'une enquête* (Paris: Nouvelles Éditions Latines, 1957) and *L'art et la pensée* (Paris: Dominique Martin Morin, 1972). The second of these has chapters on 'L'art est une parabole' (pp. 15–25), 'L'art et l'intelligence' (pp. 26–54) and 'L'art est un système de pensée' (pp. 55–70).

31. The eighth and ninth lectures on *Oeuvre d'art et technique – La couleur* were conflated to make the eighth chapter in the *Propos*, whose Sommaire lists the chapters as follows:

1. Le renouveau de l'art et du goût

2. Les conditions d'un vrai style

3. Les conditions intemporelles du beau

4. L'idéal et l'ascèse de l'art chrétien. Formalisme et rationalisme architectural dans leur rapport avec la beauté

5. Oeuvre d'art et technique – Primauté de la forme sur la lumière et la couleur

6. Oeuvre d'art et technique – Les proportions

7. Oeuvre d'art et technique – Vue d'ensemble. Genèse des formes

8. Oeuvre d'art et technique – La couleur

32. Both the dome of the Oratoire Saint-Joseph and Bellot's buildings at Saint-Benoît-du-Lac demonstrate the extensive use of reinforced concrete, and Bellot's disciples in Canada were to follow up this aspect of his work.

33. See, for example, Peter Collins, *Concrete. The Vision of a New Architecture. A Study of Auguste Perret and his Precursors* (London: Faber and Faber 1959), pp. 113–17.

34. Maritain's visit to the Isle of Wight was on 14 August 1907 and is referred to in his *Carnets de notes* (Paris: Desclée de Brouwer, 1965; paperback 1994), pp. 61–2. Its purpose was to see a mutual friend, Dom Louis Baillet (1875–1913), and to tell him of Péguy's return to Catholicism. For the Maritains' relationship with Péguy, see Pierre L'Abbé, 'Jacques Maritain and Charles Péguy: a reassessment', in John F. X. Knasis (ed.), *Jacques Maritain. The Man and his Metaphysics* (Mishawaka IN: American Maritain Association, 1988), pp. 45–52, especially p. 49.

35. Dom Charles Fitzsimons informs me that the guest book at Quarr indicates that Maritain stayed there from early August to 1 October 1914. The visit is recorded in Raïssa Maritain, *Les grandes amitiés* (Paris: Desclée de Brouwer, 1949; paperback 1993), p. 192. Other visitors to Quarr during this period include Robert Graves in 1917, as recorded in *Goodbye to All That* (rev. edn, Harmondsworth: Penguin, 1960), pp. 206–8, and Georges Bataille in 1920. Bataille described his visit in the book *L'expérience intérieure* (1954). See the English version, *Inner Experience*, tr. and intro. Leslie Anne Boldt (Albany NY: State University of New York Press, 1988), p. 58. For the context of Bataille at Quarr, see Michel Suriya, *Georges Bataille. La mort à l'œuvre* (Paris: Gallimard, 1992), p. 615. Viollet-le-Duc and Aquinas both appear in Denis Hollier, *Against Architecture. The Writings of George Bataille*, tr. Betsy Wing (Cambridge MA: MIT Press, 1989). Bataille's connections with Quarr were brought to my attention by David B. Stewart.

36. For *Art et scolastique*, see the text and notes in *Jacques et Raïssa Maritain: Oeuvres complètes*, vol. 1 (Fribourg: Éditions Universitaires, 1986), pp. 615–788. A wider view is in part 1: 'Art et Scolastique', in Bernard Hubert and Yves Floucat (eds), *Jacques Maritain et ses contemporains* (Paris: Desclée/Proost France, 1991), pp. 23–155.

37. See Augustin Savaton, *Dom Paul Delatte, Abbé de Solesmes* (Solesmes: Éditions de l'Abbaye, 1975), especially chapter 9, 'Notre-Dame de Quarr', pp. 245–83.

38. Jean Rochon, 'L'esprit d'un moine bâtisseur. Dom Paul Bellot (1876–1944)', *Chercher Dieu*, no. 16 (Spring 1994), 18. Père Rochon pointed out to me in a letter of 4 January 1996 that Dom Bellot had completed his monastic training before the appearance of Maritain's writings on *Thomisme*. Could Bellot have influenced Maritain and Dom Delatte, Père Rochon asks?

39. 'Autobiographie de Dom Bellot', typescript, fo. 3. It is dated 18 August 1931 and is inscribed 'ST OMER' (i.e. Wisques). The copy of this which I used is at Saint-Benoît-du-Lac.

40. For bibliographical information on Viollet-le-Duc's publications, see *The Foundations of Architecture. Selections from the 'Dictionnaire raisonné'*, intro. Barry Bergdoll, tr. Kenneth D. Whitehead (New York: George Braziller, 1990); and M. F. Hearn (ed.), *The Architectural Theory of Viollet-le-Duc. Readings and Commentary* (Cambridge MA: MIT Press, 1990). Even today, there is no complete English translation of the *Dictionnaire raisonné de l'architecture française*; in 1875, Charles Wethered published a translation of the article on 'restoration' as a book entitled *On Restoration*, and in 1895 George Martin Huss brought out the book *Rational Building* based on a translation of 'construction'. Bellot had access to a copy of the *Dictionnaire* in the library at Wisques; the architect Joseph Philippe (who was in charge of Bellot's office at Wisques) told me in conversation on 16 September 1991 that Bellot had inherited from his father a copy of the *Dictionnaire*, which M. Philippe then owned. Bellot uses Viollet-le-Duc's text freely, sometimes quoting directly and on other occasions paraphrasing and adding his own comments. The texts given subsequently follow the wording of the *Propos*, except for minor editorial adjustments.

41. For a structuralist interpretation of the *Dictionnaire*, see the introduction by Hubert Damisch to *Viollet-le-Duc. L'architecture raisonnée. Extraits du 'Dictionnaire de l'architecture française'* (Paris: Hermann, 1978), pp. 7–29. Damisch wrote similarly in 'The Space between', *Architectural Design*, nos 3–4 (1980), 84–9, which is a special issue (no. 27) on Viollet-le-Duc.

42. For taste ('goût'), see the *Dictionnaire*, tome 6 (1863), pp. 31–4.

43. Eliot's essay of this title (see *Selected Essays*, 3rd edn (London: Faber and Faber, 1951), pp. 13–22) is of course primarily about poetry, though the transfer to other arts is readily made.

44. For the École in the USA, see, for example, Arthur Drexler (ed.), *The Architecture of the École des Beaux-Arts* (London: Secker and Warburg, 1977), especially pp. 464–93; and for Canada see, for example, Kelly Crossman, *Architecture in Transition: From Art to Practice, 1885–1906* (Kingston & Montreal: McGill-Queen's University Press, 1987), especially pp. 85–105.

45. Tome 8 (1866), pp. 474–97. See also the section on style in Bergdoll and Whitehead, *The Foundations of Architecture*, pp. 229–63.

46. Tome 7 (1864), pp. 532–61. Viollet-le-Duc's entry on proportion is historical in tone and includes twelve diagrams.

47. Beuron is considered by Fabre in 'La décoration moderne', which forms part 5 of his *Pages d'art chrétien* (2nd edn 1926), pp. 574–82. See also the entries on the Abbey of Beuron, Beuronese Art, and Desiderius Lenz in the *New Catholic Encyclopedia* (Washington DC: The Catholic University of America, 1967). Iain Boyd Whyte assisted me in my enquiries about the Beuron School.

48. Père Jean Rochon drew my attention to this French translation, quoted in Fabre, *Pages d'art chrétien* (2nd edn 1926), pp. 578, 580.

49. Bellot says on p. 109 of the *Propos* that he first encountered *Tempelmasse* in 1910, but I have come across no edition earlier than 1912 (2nd edn 1932). There is a French translation of *Tempelmasse* among the unpublished MSS at Wisques. Père Wolff (1849–1928) was a Benedictine and a member of the Beuron congregation, though from the abbey at Prague.

50. Lenz and Wolff were brought together by Nikolaus Pevsner, 'Quarr and Bellot', *The Architectural Review*, vol. 141, no. 842 (April 1967), 309. A letter from David B. Stewart in response to this article, in which he refers to French precedent for Bellot's brickwork, is in *The Architectural Review*, vol. 142, no. 845 (July 1967), 83.

51. Ghyka's books include *L'esthétique des proportions dans la nature et dans les arts* (Paris: Gallimard, 1927); *Le nombre d'or*, 2 vols (Paris: Gallimard, 1931); and *Un essai sur le rythme* (Paris: Gallimard, 1938).

52. Jean Petit, *Le Corbusier lui-même* (Geneva: Rousseau, 1970), p. 74, under the year '1931'. For further comments, see Le Corbusier and Pierre Jeanneret, *Oeuvre complète, 1929–1934*, 4th edn (1946), p. 117. See generally Charles Jencks, *Le Corbusier and the Tragic View of Architecture*, rev. edn (Harmondsworth: Penguin, 1987), pp. 113, 126–9.

53. For Le Corbusier's answer to Senger, see *Le Corbusier Talks with Students from the Schools of Architecture*, tr. Pierre Chase (New York: Orion, 1961), pp. 77–84, originally published as *Entretien avec les étudiants des écoles d'architecture* (Paris: Denoël 1943). Prominence is given to these arguments in Maximilien Gauthier, *Le Corbusier; ou l'architecture au service de l'homme* (Paris: Denoël, 1944), in which there are chapters on *Le cheval de Troie du Bolchevisme* (pp. 175–98) and another entitled 'Umbdenstock, Mauclair et Cie' (pp. 199–218). Le Corbusier counter-attacked in his own book *Croisade, ou le crépuscule des académies* (1933), which answered both Senger and Professor Gustave Umbdenstock of the École des Beaux-Arts, who had launched a campaign against Le Corbusier. Umbdenstock (1866–1940) had been a student at

the École des Beaux-Arts with Bellot, and later became a well-known patron and member of the Académie. See the references to Le Corbusier in Donald Drew Egbert, *The Beaux-Arts Tradition in French Architecture, illustrated by the Grands Prix de Rome*, ed. David van Zanten (Princeton NJ: Princeton University Press, 1980), notably p. 76.

54. Bellot's lecture on *Le renouveau de l'art et du goût* contains no further reference to Le Corbusier, nor does he appear elsewhere in the *Propos*. However, the architect is mentioned in the coda to the text of lecture 4 as published in the *Revue trimestrielle canadienne* and *Liturgical Arts* in French and English respectively. Here, the 'formalists' are represented by Viollet-le-Duc and the 'rationalists' by Le Corbusier. See *Revue trimestrielle canadienne*, vol. 20, no. 77 (March 1934), 11, and *Liturgical Arts*, vol. 4, no. 4 (1935), 159, and note 60 below.

55. *Relations*, vol. 9, no. 102 (June 1949), 170–1. This and subsequent reviews were brought to my notice by Claude Bergeron.

56. *La revue Dominicaine*, vol. 55, no. 2 (October 1949), 92.

57. *Les carnets Viatoriens*, vol. 14, no. 4 (October 1949), 312.

58. *Liaison*, vol. 3, no. 26 (June 1949), 351–2.

59. The MSS at Wisques contain the unpublished texts of lectures and talks on many topics given by Bellot to pastors, teachers, engineers, former students at the École des Beaux-Arts, and others.

60. In chronological order, these articles are: 'Questions du jour. Où va notre architecture religieuse?', *Almanach catholique français pour 1933* (Paris: Librairie Bloud and Gay, 1933), pp. 166–7. English translation as 'Where is our architecture heading?' in Geoffrey Simmins (ed.), *Documents in Canadian Architecture* (Peterborough ON: Broadview Press, 1992), pp. 174–6.

'L'idéal et l'ascèse de l'art chrétien. Formalisme et rationalisme architectural dans leur rapport avec la beauté', *Revue trimestrielle canadienne*, vol. 20, no. 77 (March 1934), 1–11. English translation as 'The ideal and discipline of Christian art', *Liturgical Arts*, vol. 4, no. 4 (1935), 153–9. Chapter 4 of the *Propos* is based on these articles, though it omits material on pp. 9–11 of the French version, and on pp. 157–9 of the English version which refers to Péguy, Frank Lloyd Wright and Le Corbusier. Material from Péguy quoted here is included in chapter 1 of the *Propos*, p. 36.

'Réflexions sur l'architecture', *L'artisan liturgique*, vol. 9, no. 39 (October–December 1935), 795–813, reprinted in two parts in *Le béton armé*, nos 336–7 (February and March 1936), 1,368–78 and 1,384–96. The section 'La couleur' here has affinities with chapter 8 of the *Propos*.

'Voies de l'architecture', *La Métropole*, 28–29 May 1939, pp. 9–10. This article contains material from chapter 1 of the *Propos*.

'Art et tradition. Propos d'un ouvrier logeur du Bon Dieu', based on a lecture delivered in May 1940 to the Alliance Française and published in the *Revue trimestrielle canadienne*, vol. 26, no. 104 (December 1940), 357–84. This is an extensive statement which includes Bellot's views on the artistic tradition of the Catholic church in Canada, the promotion of the arts, and issues of national identity for French-Canadians. I am grateful to Charlotte Ellis for her comments on these publications.

61. For the work of Bellot's disciples in Canada, see the sources cited in note 16 above, particularly the forthcoming essay by Claude Bergeron and Nicole Tardif-Painchaud. The work of Dufresne was the subject of three articles by Bellot (the first under the pseudonym 'Denis') using the same text: 'Sainte-Thérèse de l'Enfant Jésus (près de

Beauport). L'heureux résultat d'une révolution', *L'action catholique* (Quebec), vol. 1, no. 32 (1 August 1937), pp. 1,7; 'Sainte-Thérèse de Beauport. L'heureux résultat d'une révolution', *Almanach de l'action sociale catholique*, vol. 22 (1938), 64–6; and 'Sainte-Thérèse de Beauport. A. Dufresne, architecte. Le résultat d'une révolution', *Architecture, bâtiment, construction*, vol. 2, no. 18 (October 1947), 32–40.

Also in Canada, Bellot prepared designs with Ernest Cormier for Le Grand Séminaire de Québec, but these were superseded.

From 1939, whilst he was in Canada, Bellot's church of the Immaculate Conception in Porto, Portugal, was being built. It was not completed until 1947.

62. Dom Côté, unlike Bellot, was fully qualified as an architect in Canada, having trained at the École des Beaux-Arts in Montreal. He sent drawings of Saint-Benoît-du-Lac to M. Philippe in France and visited him several times. Père Rochon told me in conversation in June 1994 that M. Philippe suggested many alterations to Dom Côté's designs, including the more extensive use of reinforced concrete.

63. Notably at the abbey of Saint-Benoît-du-Lac, with the publication of an issue of *Chercher Dieu*, no. 16 (Spring 1994), devoted to 'Notre église monastique', with an article by Père Jean Rochon, 'L'esprit d'un moine bâtisseur. Dom Paul Bellot (1876–1944)', pp. 10–39. Also Dom Guy-Marie Oury, 'Le cinquantenaire de la mort de Dom Paul Bellot', *L'ami de Saint-Benoît-du-Lac*, no. 84 (July 1994), 10–11; and Bruno Lafleur, 'Les adieux de Dom Bellot', ibid., pp. 11–12. Felicitously, the year 1994 witnessed the completion of Dan Hanganu's church. See 'Building the House of God. The Monastery of Saint-Benoît-du-Lac', a video prepared by the University of Calgary in 1994, with a text by Geoffrey Simmins.

64. Peter F. Anson, 'Dom Paul Bellot, OSB (1876–1944)', *Pax*, vol. 31, no. 232 (Autumn 1944), 109–16, reprinted in *Liturgical Arts*, vol. 13, no. 3 (May 1945), 50 a. Anson, a Catholic convert, published extensively on architecture and Christianity. For an admirable synopsis of his life, see Tudor Edwards' obituary of him in *The Times*, 19 June 1975, p. 14.

65. Nikolaus Pevsner, 'Quarr and Bellot', *The Architectural Review*, vol. 141, no. 842 (April 1967), 307–10.

66. For van der Laan, see Richard Padovan, *Dom Hans van der Laan. Modern Primitive* (Amsterdam: Architectura and Natura Press, 1994). Van der Laan's buildings are in many ways the antithesis of those of Dom Bellot, indicating that the Benedictine rule can lead to a variety of architectural expressions. Van der Laan met Bellot, and through him encountered the golden section as used by Desiderius Lenz and the Beuron School. 'The secret of [Bellot's] art', wrote van der Laan in a letter to Richard Padovan, 'lay in the golden section, and he had long ago had a set-square made in that proportion, which he used in all his designs instead of the normal sixty-degree one. His elevations in particular were based on super-subtle diagrams derived from it. But when he tried to convince me of its supreme value, I failed to see what it had to do with architecture and it seemed to me just another arbitrary mathematical formula.' Elsewhere, van der Laan notes his opposition to the theatricality of Dom Bellot's church planning (as at Quarr and Oosterhout) in which there is 'a sequence of three spaces: a space for the congregation, one for the monks' choir and one for the ceremonies around the altar'. Van der Laan 'quickly set [himself] against this arrangement, which turns the liturgy into a spectacle rather than a collective action'.

See Padovan, *Van der Laan*, pp. 85–7, 144.

SUPPLEMENTARY NOTE

Since the original publication of this study in April 1996 in the *British Journal of Canadian Studies* (volume 11, number 1 (1996), pp. 90–124), the exhibition 'Dom Bellot: Moine-Architecte' has been held at the Institut Français d'Architecture in Paris from 13 June to 7 September 1996.

Accompanying the exhibition was the book *Dom Bellot: Moine-Architecte (1876–1944)*, edited by Maurice Culot and Martin Meade, with contemporary photographs by Dominique Delaunay (Paris: Éditions Norma, 1996). This contains on pp. 97–113 the article 'Dom Bellot au Canada', by Claude Bergeron and Nicole Tardif-Painchaud, referred to in Notes 16 and 61 above.

INDEX OF PERSONS